Weight Loss Smoothies

33 Healthy and Delicious Smoothie Recipes to Boost

Your Metabolism, Burn Fat and Lose Weight Fast

Sara Elliott Price

Published in The USA by:

Success Life Publishing

125 Thomas Burke Dr.

Hillsborough, NC 27278

Copyright © 2015 by Sara Elliott Price

ISBN-10: 1514327203

Table of Contents

Introduction

I want to thank you for downloading, *"Weight Loss Smoothies: 33 Healthy and Delicious Smoothie Recipes to Boost Your Metabolism, Burn Fat, and Lose Weight Fast!"*

By deciding to download this book you have taken the first step to achieving the physique you've always dreamed of.

Throughout this book you will discover why smoothies may be the greatest weapon in your weight loss battle. Not only will you lose weight and the excess inches around your waist, you will also gain new found energy and add life to your years.

As we all know, proper nutrition is the foundation needed to start your weight loss journey. Smoothies can give you that nutrition in a very delicious way! The word 'overweight' doesn't have to be in your future and even if you have a few pounds to lose right now, there is a good chance that the goodness locked inside fresh fruits and veggies can melt the fat away fast.

Are you ready to look in the mirror and see a toned body and firm skin? How about having a pep in your step with loads of energy? Or maybe you just want to lose a few pounds and halt the aging process. It doesn't matter how much weight or inches you need to lose because smoothies can take you there.

All you need to do is follow the advice in this book and I promise only good things can come from it.

Today most people take a pill for everything or look for some magic potion that will solve their weight issues overnight. Most people don't understand that healing and weight loss start from within. Quit giving your body the bad stuff and feed it the stuff it needs and you will naturally move towards your perfect body. Most people never know what it truly feels like to love who they are. They go through life feeling "OK." But I want you to feel **AMAZING**! The nutrition from fresh produce is the key to giving you the body you've always wanted.

Jumpstart your weight loss by diving head first into the following pages. If you read the information, understand it and apply it in your daily life I have no doubts you will look and feel like a brand new, better version of yourself a month from now.

Thanks again for downloading this book, I hope it serves you well on your weight loss journey.

Chapter 1: The Wonderful Smoothie

Just ask anyone who has battled with excess weight at some point in their lives: losing weight is not an easy task at all! Well what would you say if I told you that there was a sure-fire way you could lose all those bulging mounds of fat and reduce the strain on your poor knees while lounging in your garden with a big chilled glass of delicious goodness? Yes, I know it sounds too good to be true, but it is actually true.

There are many different types of smoothies and most recipes you will find are very tasty and delicious. Believe it or not, people even use them as an alternative to weight loss diets.

Green smoothies, for instance, have been all the rage since being discovered by raw food pioneer, Victoria Boutenko. Which is surprising for most people, considering they wouldn't think that a smoothie that looks like pond water would be tasty.

Hey, you could forgive most people for being skeptical. I mean let's face it, even if you live in a cave far from every trace of civilization you probably know that green vegetables are one of the best foods for people looking to lose weight and also generally live a healthy life. However, you probably also know that they are hard to force down because they often taste horrible!

The good thing about smoothies, however, is that you can sneak in some vegetables that you wouldn't consume otherwise—without even tasting them! An example of this would be a green smoothie. They are made by blending a combination of green, leafy vegetables and fruits to create one of the healthiest food combinations you can imagine. The best part about green smoothies is that they contain such a vast array of nutrients.

So what are the best types of vegetables to use in your smoothies? Well in truth cruciferous vegetables like cabbage, cauliflower, broccoli and Brussels sprouts are fine, but when it comes to smoothies for weight loss, you want leafy greens. Examples include kale, lettuce, celery, spinach, collards, chard, basil, cilantro and parsley.

Oh and just in case you are feeling adventurous and thinking of picking non-traditional greens for your smoothie, you should know to *never* put potato leaves, eggplant leaves, tomato leaves or bell pepper leaves in your smoothie. These belong to the nightshade family and are, frankly, naturally poisonous. I'm not exaggerating. They will make you sick if ingested.

Smoothies are a wonderful source of more nutrients than you

could imagine and their benefits are so numerous that if you drink them every day you may never get sick again! Really, when it comes to smoothies, four words: detox, beautify, energize and slim!

Chapter 2: Weight Loss Smoothies

There have been many trials and studies that have shown that people do lose weight with smoothies. When it comes down to it, you can't help wondering what exactly it is about smoothies that cause weight loss. Especially when some recipes are so tasty they seem downright sinful.

Well for starters, most smoothies are extremely low in calories whilst providing the body with enzymes, vitamins, phytonutrients, and minerals; depending of course on what you put in them.

Smoothies are the best drink of choice before and after workouts because they restore lost energy, replace vitamins and leave you feeling refreshed.

By their very nature, smoothies offer you pure, unadulterated nutrition—depending of course on the fruits, veggies and other supplements you add to them.

Green smoothies on their part are great for weight loss because unlike juices where you get all the vitamins and minerals with no fiber—green smoothies aren't stripped of their beneficial fiber. Not to mention, green smoothies have a balanced sugar profile. Because of their high green veggie to fruit ratio they are not metabolized as quickly as plain fruit smoothies which ordinarily have a higher sugar content. Also, because the produce has already been broken down by your blender, it makes it that much easier for your body to digest, thereby conserving your energy.

Some people scoff at the idea that digestion takes any energy from us; well think back to the last time your stomach was Thanksgiving-dinner-full and tell me if you felt like embarking on a 2 mile run immediately after. Thought so!

Most people have eating disorders because in a bid to lose weight or keep in shape, they tend to avoid meals. This cheats the body of necessary nutrients and makes them either scarecrow thin or just plain sick enough to bring almost every doctor in the country running to their bed side. That's where smoothies come in handy.

They have enough fiber so that you feel satiated without you so much as eating solid food—and no, I'm not telling you not to. Smoothies are extraordinarily filling which is what makes you reduce your food intake, yet have an adequate infuse of nutrients.

Smoothies also create weight loss because they have a high mineral content which includes everything from calcium, to magnesium, to phosphorous. They work to help you lose weight, burn calories faster and also give you the energy needed to workout faster, longer and harder. The thing about smoothies is that you don't necessarily have to wait until you are pushing 40 to develop a taste for them as they are often so surprisingly tasty that even kids would be hard pressed to resist them.

Now just to lay all the cards on the table, not every weight loss smoothie tastes fantastic. Because let's face it, taste is more often than not determined by whatever you put in them. So sometimes you have to play around with the recipes and decide what works for you.

No matter how great you think strawberries are, some people detest them and some think of them as an acquired taste. So keep an open mind and even when you find several different recipes you like, keep changing them up every now and then, as it is never best to stick to the same few recipes all the time. Especially if you are trying to lose weight. The reason for this is that you may get bored, your taste buds may protest and more importantly, you would be limiting the amount of nutrients you get exposed to. For instance, even if they are both green, you can't seriously expect to get the exact same nutrients from kale and spinach!

The greatest cause of excess weight is our sweet tooth—no

matter how much we hate to admit it. Smoothies create weight loss by helping curb your cravings for sweet things: yes, believe it or not, sipping on a healthy, tasty, fiber-packed green or fruit smoothie not only fills you up and lessens actual hunger; it also takes care of your sweet tooth.

Smoothies also detoxify, flushing harmful waste out of your system and helping your body heal and revitalize itself. Smoothies also take care of bloating thus making you slimmer automatically.

Exercise remains the best weight loss method known to man and while I am currently studiously ignoring your groans of displeasure, let me just inform you that healthy smoothies not only increase your stamina, they also make you a lot more inclined to work out. Now if that isn't a sure fire way to lose weight, I don't know what is. Exercise is a whole lot easier if you are incorporating smoothies into your diet because you feel ten times lighter and it is that much easier to carry yourself. Plus, the different nutrients coursing through your veins means you burn calories faster than you normally would.

What most people do not realize is that no matter how much or how little they eat, if they aren't consuming nutrients, their metabolism shuts down and their body goes into stress mode. This means they can't lose weight no matter how much they try. Smoothies provide your body with all sorts of much needed nutrients which in turn keep your metabolism awake and raring to go.

Most ingredients used in smoothies are packed with fiber which means they often digest slowly. Smoothies tend to flush the digestive system quickly, giving the body little or no time to store up fat. When you start to burn more fat than you store, the logical result is weight loss. At the same time, when people are lacking in nutrients, they tend to find it just a tad harder to lose weight because their metabolism drops like a rock. This explains why healthy smoothies work like a charm. Smoothies are known to speed up metabolism and also provide your body with much needed nutrients which means you get to shed a great deal of weight just from drinking smoothies made with the right ingredients.

Chapter 3: Revitalize Your Health

Smoothies deliver tons of nutrients to the body in a short period of time. Now even if you are one of the alarmingly few people who actually like green vegetables, I am willing to bet you rarely take the time to properly chew the leaves. What I mean is, raw green vegetables are probably the healthiest food on the planet but no matter how often you eat them, they probably won't do you much good if you don't chew them well enough to rupture the cell walls and expose the nutrients within them. Green smoothies are already blended thoroughly which means the nutrients from the indigestible cellulose are released beforehand by the blender and are made readily available to your body and digestive system as soon as you take one tiny sip!

Okay so just in case you didn't know, most foods of modern civilization are a whole lot more acidic than are good for your system; and yes, the list would include your caffeine, cheese, etc. Smoothies are, in general, a very alkalizing food. They are able to efficiently neutralize acids in your body. Blueberries for instance are a common ingredient in smoothies and they contain numerous wonderful properties—one of which is a chemical known as pterostilbene which could help prevent colon cancer.

Healthy fruit or green vegetable smoothies also boost

immunity and make people less prone to diseases; even chronic diseases. I mean, they are known for being high in foliate which guards against heart diseases and also cancer. Now I'm no doctor, but even when people already have established medical conditions, fresh fruit and vegetables have been known to turn their prognosis around! Note though, that I am certainly not advocating relying on them as medicine despite how potent they can be. I am just saying that when it comes to weight loss, it doesn't get much healthier than smoothies!

The American Cancer Society thinks eating five to nine servings of fruits and green veggies per day helps to prevent cancer and other diseases and let's face it, no matter how much of a fruit freak you are, stuffing down nine servings of fruits and green veggies per day isn't easy. But with smoothies, you consume more than enough fruits and veggies without even noticing.

Healthy smoothies are packed with chlorophyll which purifies the blood and rejuvenates the body which is far healthier than their supplemental counterparts. Another added bonus is that the fiber in smoothies keeps your digestive system operating smoothly. In other words, if you keep clean on the inside you'll radiate health.

Chapter 4: Delectable Smoothie Recipes

There are a variety of recipes for healthy weight loss smoothies and most people tend to go ahead and experiment with the fruits and green veggies they have in order to decide what works best for them. You should try to make certain that whatever recipe you use has bananas or mangoes as a base fruit. Because apart from being sweet enough to mask the taste of greens altogether, they both help give your drink that actual smoothie texture.

Of course it goes without saying that water or other non-dairy liquid is also generally a great and necessary addition to your smoothie. Apart from the fact that your body needs it to stay hydrated, your blender needs it if the blades are going to work properly. You could choose to sweeten your smoothie by throwing in some honey, agave nectar or other natural sweetener or depending on the smoothie perhaps some other sweet fruit. The following recipes will help you shed excess weight and rejuvenate your body!

Blueberry Green Smoothie

The blueberry green smoothie is made from blueberry, bananas and spinach or kale. Now just in case you didn't know, research has shown that blueberries contain certain nutrients that are significant in battling belly fat. According to researcher, Mitchell Seymour of the University of Michigan's Cardio Protection Research Laboratory, when studies were conducted on test subjects using the fruit, "Blueberry intake affected genes related to fat-burning and storage."

Blueberries are high in Vitamins C and E, anthocyanins and phenolics. Bananas are higher in calories than most other fruits but they provide energy and nutrition without fat, which is why they are great for weight loss.

The Blueberry Green Smoothie requires:

1 cup of blueberries
1 banana
2 big handfuls of spinach
Almond milk as needed

Raspberry Coconut Smoothie

Raspberries are chock full of essential nutrients as I'm sure you know. They are also very low in calories and fat but high in fiber, which is a testament to their weight loss potential. Spinach is basically the go-to vegetable for weight loss and has an encouragingly low-calorie content which has been pegged at just 7 calories per cup.

The ingredients for this smoothie include:

1 cup of raspberries

1/3 cup of coconut flakes

2 big handfuls of spinach

1 cup of water

Ice cubes

Peaches and Spinach Green Smoothie

I could tell you that Spinach is rich in just about everything from iron, to folate to magnesium, to calcium, to antioxidants, and that would be very true; but that doesn't even do this wonderful green justice! Spinach is insanely filling and one of the best foods for weight loss.

If that's not enough to have you reaching for this smoothie, then you should also know that peaches are a natural source of Vitamin A and C and are very high on the list of weight-loss foods. And honey, sweet as it is, triggers metabolic changes that ensure your body won't crave sugar. Talk about a win/win!

This power-packed smoothie includes:

1 peach fruit
2 handfuls of spinach
¼ cup of raw oats
1 cup of water
1 tablespoon of honey
Ice cubes

Watermelon Smoothie

The water content in watermelon accounts for why it should be one of the first weight loss foods to add into a smoothie. It's low in calories and fat and thankfully requires little ingredients to thoroughly enjoy sipping your glass.

This recipe includes the following:

6 cups of seedless watermelon

1 cup of lemon sherbet

6 ice cubes

Creamy Coconut Green Smoothie

Clementines are tiny citrus fruits very much like tangerines and yes, they are great for weight loss. Apart from being juicy and succulent, they are also filling and full of water. When you include them in your green smoothie, you will stay full for much longer.

The ingredients for this smoothie include:

3 large Clementine

¼ cup of coconut milk

1 banana

2 cups of spinach

Ice cubes

Pineapple and Spinach Green Smoothie

So this has got to be one of the tastiest green smoothies around. It's so good even kids will be screaming for it. The pineapple and banana are an amazing combination taste wise, but the pineapple has a special enzyme that makes it even better for weight loss. The enzyme bromelain in pineapple actually breaks down protein into its individual amino acids. As I'm sure you can imagine this can both give you energy and also help you lose weight.

Blend the following together:

1 fresh pineapple
½ banana
2 handfuls of spinach
2 cups of water
Ice cubes

**Mixed Berry Smoothie**

If you've been doing your homework, then you know berries are very good for weight loss whether they be raspberries, blueberries, or strawberries. This mixed berry smoothie is easy to make, very tasty and healthy too.

Simply blend together:

1 cup of frozen berries

½ cup of non-fat vanilla or plain yogurt

Ice cubes

Peachy Green Smoothie

Kale is one of the 'big boys in town' when it comes to weight loss. It is thought to be even more potent than spinach. Speaking of, wherever the recipe calls for spinach, you could use kale, and vice versa. Kale is so high in fiber, it's amazing; it is a dieter's 'dream food' what with its startling combination of minerals, phytonutrients, and vitamins. It's a wonderful source of beta-carotene, calcium and trace minerals.

There are several types of kale like the Russian kale, the curly red kale, the curly green kale and the Lacinato kale but when it comes to green smoothies, you want the curly green kale! On a side note, strawberries are known for stimulating metabolism and suppressing appetite; now if that doesn't spell weight loss, I don't know what does!

For this you will need the following:

1 peach
1 banana
1 cup of kale
1 scoop of whey protein
6 frozen strawberries
Almond milk as needed
Ice cubes

Mocha Smoothie

Yes, I said 'Mocha'. You may officially begin salivating now! While there is nothing raw about this smoothie, it's totally delicious and promotes weight loss.

The caffeine in this smoothie reduces hunger and increases energy. It's a great pre-workout meal, that will let you workout harder for longer. Nothing helps weight loss more than excess energy when you workout.

The recipe includes:

½ cup of low-fat vanilla yogurt

1 shot of espresso

2 teaspoons of cocoa powder

Almond milk as needed

4 small ice cubes

Holy Basil Smoothie

Holy basil is a refreshing change from spinach and kale and that's not all; basil helps in reducing excess weight. It does this by helping to renew energy and decreasing the cortisol levels in your blood. Holy basil is a king among herbs and you simply cannot go wrong adding it to your diet.

Get the following for this smoothie:

2 handfuls of holy basil leaves

1 apple fruit

1 ripe orange fruit

Water as needed

Ice cubes

Green Drink

This is actually the green smoothie to beat all green smoothies and it's one most stars swear by, just ask Dr Oz! It has enough nutrients to make any dietician happy and also a healthy combination of greens; see the celery, cucumber and parsley.

The high fiber content of this smoothie means your stomach will feel full for far longer. And the vibrant green color is a sign of chlorophyll. Chlorophyll boosts energy levels, oxygenates the blood and flushes out harmful toxins from the body!

For this recipe you need:

2 cups of spinach

½ a cucumber

¼ of a head of celery

½ bunch of parsley

1 bunch of mint

3 carrots

2 apples

¼ orange

1 lime fruit

¼ lemon

1 slice of pineapple

4 – 6 ice cubes

Vitamin C Smoothie

Strawberries are not just pretty red fruits everyone eats with whipped cream; they are Nature's gift to mankind. Strawberries promote the production of two hormones known as adiponectin and leptin both of which are metabolic fat burning hormones. This means with every strawberry you eat, you increase your metabolism and lose excess body fat.

Grab these few ingredients:

2 oranges

½ cantaloupe

1 cup of strawberries

3 tomatoes

Ice cubes

Papaya Smoothie

Apple is great for weight loss, as are bananas but when you throw in papaya into the mix, it's like loading a gun and pointing it at the head of excess fat! Papaya is very popular because of its high content of the enzyme papain, which has been shown to help break down protein (and is consequently popularly used as a meat tenderizer).

Now just before you start blending, make certain to include the banana in the mix as they tend to give your smoothie the right texture as well as sweeten the smoothie. Apple suppresses appetite to the point where studies have shown that people who eat just 1 apple before meals, eat 185 calories less than normal during the meal; go apple!

Blend these ingredients:

¼ of a whole papaya
½ banana
½ green apple
Ice cubes

Super Energy Smoothie

Like the name suggests, this smoothie is an amazing source of energy that puts all energy drinks to shame! Just in case you're wondering what energy has to do with weight loss, let me ask you a question. When was the last time you were really tired and still felt like going on a 5 mile run? Exactly! With more energy your workouts become fun and of course more weight loss inducing.

The ingredients for the recipe include:

¼ of a medium sized pineapple

¼ of a medium sized watermelon

1 cup of coconut water

3 handfuls of baby spinach

1 cup of blueberries

2 green apples or 2 bananas

Ice cubes

Paradise Smoothie

Yeah the name also makes me think of warm, lazy afternoons on a sandy beach with colourful scarves flying around. As exotic drinks go, this smoothie gets the big hat! It contains seemingly simple ingredients but their benefits especially to your weight are super-amazing!

Blend the following and *bon appétit*!

1 medium sized ripe peach

2 tablespoons of Hass Avocado

1/3 cup of strawberries

¾ cup of fat-free yogurt

3 tablespoons of 100% pomegranate juice

1 tablespoon of grapeseed oil

1 teaspoon of pure vanilla extract

Ice cubes

The Glowing Green Smoothie

This smoothie is courtesy of Kimberly Snyder and she and all her clients swear by it for weight loss, better skin and good health. The romaine lettuce does wonders for the body with its high water content and even higher doses of fiber and minerals. When you factor in the celery, spinach, lemon and the apple in this smoothie, you would understandably not have a reason to look at another smoothie ever again.

For this recipe blend together:

1 ½ cups of water

1 head of romaine lettuce

3 to 4 stalks of organic celery

2 handfuls of spinach

1 organic apple

1 organic pear

1 organic banana

¼ cup of fresh lemon juice

4-6 ice cubes

1/3 bunch of cilantro

1/3 bunch of parsley

Clementine Grapefruit Smoothie

Grapefruits are amazing for weight loss whether alone or in a smoothie. Grapefruits contain compounds that help lower insulin and help you eat less. This fruit will kick-start your digestion and the naringenin content helps the liver break down fat while increasing insulin sensitivity.

Gather the following ingredients:

1 clementine

¼ of a grapefruit

½ a lemon

1 apple

2 dates

1 small mango

1 tablespoon of nutmeg

¼ tablespoon of pumpkin seeds

¼ of a celery

1 cup of coconut milk

2 bananas

1 orange

4-6 ice cubes

The Wellness Warrior Smoothie

Come on, blueberries, banana, spirulina, romaine lettuce, goji berry, maca, chia and hemp, all in a glass; how could anyone not lose weight with this one? If there were ever a superfood smoothie it would be this!

This deliciously rich green smoothie includes:

3 leaves of romaine lettuce

1 cup of coconut water

1 small frozen banana

A small handful of goji berries

A handful of blueberries

1 teaspoon of hemp seeds

1 teaspoon of chia seeds

1 teaspoon bee pollen

1 teaspoon maca powder

1 teaspoon spirulina

Ice cubes

**Killer Kale**

Kale has been shown to be one of the best greens you can include in your diet—full of minerals and chlorophyll. It can be slightly bitter to those new to consuming greens, but you'll quickly come to love the taste. The hemp seeds and almond butter give you a nice bit of fat and protein to keep you full for hours.

For this simple smoothie includes:

1 ½ C almond milk

1 ½ T almond butter

1 banana, frozen

2 C kale

1 T hemp seeds

Berry Carrot

This smoothie may not look as good as it tastes, but remember: looks can be deceiving. Chia seeds are extremely high in omega-3's. This whole smoothie is a fiber powerhouse—which is excellent for weight loss. If you thought carrots were good for the eyes you probably never realized that spinach with its Lutein content makes it just as good, if not better for your eyesight.

For this smoothie gather the following:

½ C almond milk

½ C water

1 carrot

2 C spinach

½ C frozen berries

1 T chia seeds

½ t Stevia (optional)

Minty Fresh

This smoothie really will make you feel fresh! If you've ever chewed a piece of mint gum, you'll understand what I mean. Swiss chard is an excellent source of calcium and potassium. The pineapple makes an excellent addition as its bromelain content helps to break down proteins. This means if you have excess protein in your digestive system it can help to break it down and speed up your weight loss.

To make this smoothie you will need:

1 bunch swiss chard

½ C raspberries, frozen

½ C pineapple, frozen

½ C peaches, frozen

3 T mint leaves

¼ C orange juice

Peachy Oat Smoothie

If you're looking for a hearty breakfast but you're sick of the same old thing try this smoothie! It is packed full of complex carbohydrates and the chia seeds give it a thickness that when combined with the oatmeal will keep you sustained for hours.

***It is best to let the chia seeds and oats soak overnight in the fridge with ¼ C almond milk and blend the next day with the remaining ingredients.

For this smoothie you will need:

½ C rolled oats
1/3 C plain yogurt
¼ C almond milk for soaking
¼ C almond milk for blending
1 small peach
½ medium banana
1 T chia seeds
Pinch of salt

Cacao Peanut Butter Milkshake

This simple smoothie is so delicious you'll want it for dessert! In fact, I have it nearly every night as my after dinner treat. No added sugars, a decent amount of protein and fat, with just the right amount of chocolate-y goodness. No one will ever guess this is healthy!

To make this you will need:

1 medium banana, frozen
1 T peanut butter
1 C almond milk
1 T cacao powder
½ tsp. vanilla extract

Strawberry Peach Oatmeal

This is another great breakfast smoothie! High in complex carbohydrates because of the oatmeal, high in protein because of the Greek yogurt and a nice dose of omega-3's thanks to the chia seeds. Add in the vitamin C that you get from the fruit and you have yourself a well-rounded, filling breakfast.

For this smoothie you will need:

½ peach (3-4 slices), frozen

6-8 strawberries, frozen

½ C rolled oats (cooked and cooled)

½ C plain Greek yogurt

¼ C orange juice

1 T chia seeds

Coconut Lime

The taste of this smoothie makes me want to sit by the beach on a hot summer's day. Coconut milk is pretty awesome. Besides being delicious it has some amazing benefits. The Lauric acid in coconut milk converts into monolaurin in the body, which is an antiviral and antibacterial. This means coconut milk has the ability to destroy a host of infections and viruses in the body. Add that to the fact mango is very high in vitamin c and you have a smoothie that can keep you well all summer long.

For this smoothie grab the following:

½ banana, frozen
½ mango
1/3 C coconut milk
Juice of 1 lime
Pinch of ground cardamom

Pink Drink

I love the color of this smoothie/juice hybrid. In this smoothie you get a nice little boost of veggies with a sweet and tart flavor. Grapefruit is great for weight loss. It contains a compound that lowers insulin, which happens to be the "fat storing" hormone. Less insulin means less fat around the middle that is one of the biggest problem areas people have. Add to that the cancer fighting phytochemicals and this is a smoothie I use on a regular basis.

For this smoothie you will need:

½ English cucumber, peeled and diced
½ small raw beet, peeled and diced
1 apple, cored and diced
Juice of 1 large grapefruit

Mojito

This smoothie contains a higher amount of fat than a lot of the recipes here. Fat does not always equal weight gain; in fact, it can actually help you lose weight. Fat simply has more calories per gram and if you don't pay attention you may consume too many calories elsewhere.

Fat halts or reduces the amount of insulin your body needs at one time, meaning you have less insulin in your blood stream. Hemp seeds are one of the few plant sources that contain all the essential amino acids in abundance and are very high in omega 3's. This is a wonderful dinner smoothie if you are too tired to cook.

For this smoothie you will need:

1 C coconut water
2 T hemp seeds
½-1 teaspoon spirulina
2 T fresh lime juice
½ avocado
1 banana, frozen
2 dates, pitted
1 handful mint leaves

Vanilla ginger

You may be surprised at how much flavor one smoothie can contain. Ginger and other spices can actually help you lose weight in an interesting way. They decrease and remove inflammation from the body. When you are inflamed your "master weight loss hormone" Leptin isn't as effective.

Being overweight actually creates inflammation on top of all the other inflammatory things in our lifestyles. In order for Leptin to work properly we need to lose the inflammation. So why not spice up your life with this smoothie and begin to not only lose weight but also notice all sorts of health problems begin to disappear.

For this smoothie you will need:

1 banana, frozen

1 C almond milk

½ teaspoon powdered ginger

½ teaspoon cinnamon

1 dash each of cardamom, cloves and nutmeg

¼ teaspoon vanilla

<u>Silk Chocolate</u>

This smoothie is an excellent transition from regular dairy milk. The avocado gives it just the right amount of creamy texture and a nice dose of healthy monounsaturated fats. This recipe will make you realize you don't need dairy to enjoy delicious chocolate milk.

For this you will need:

¼ C coconut milk

3 dates, pitted

¼ avocado

1 T cacao powder

Peanut Butter Bomb

If you are like me then you love peanut butter. I think after trying this smoothie once it will become your new go to snack when you need to get your peanut butter fix. The chia seeds in this smoothie give you a large boost of omega 3's which help balance out the omega 6 in the peanut butter. Not only that but chia seeds are very high in soluble fiber.

When chia seeds get wet they start to gel and expand. Not only does this create a wonderful texture for your smoothie but it also means it will move throughout your body and pull things along. It will help jump start your digestion in other words, which is a major benefit for weight loss.

For this recipe grab the following:

1 C almond milk
1 banana, frozen
½ T chia seeds
½ T peanut butter
¼ teaspoon vanilla extract

**Flax Spinach**

Are you looking for a high protein smoothie? Then look no further! The greek yogurt and peanut butter give you loads of protein while the flaxseed gives you a big dose of omega 3's. This one is my go to pre workout smoothie that gives me the energy to exercise in a way that promotes easy weight loss.

For this smoothie you will need:

½ C vanilla Greek yogurt

1 C almond milk

1 T peanut butter

2 C spinach

1 banana, frozen

3 strawberries

1 teaspoon flaxseed

Blue and Black

This smoothie is just plain ol' delicious. A simple way to get your greens in while enjoying some sweet berry goodness. Spinach and berries are some of the best foods to help reduce inflammation, which as we discussed earlier is needed to induce weight loss. Enjoy this smoothie anytime you feel like a healthy, sweet treat.

You will need the following:

2-3 C spinach

1 C almond milk

1 banana, frozen

¼ C blueberries, frozen

¼ C blackberries, frozen

A Shot in The Arm

We should strive to get our daily vitamins and minerals through a healthy diet. The papaya will give you a huge boost of vitamin C to keep your immune system healthy and keep sickness and disease away. The spinach and kale give you a healing dose of calcium and magnesium, while the banana and apple give you a shot of energy!

Blend the following together:

1 C papaya

½ C kale

½ C spinach

½ banana

½ green apple

Chapter 5: Enhance Your Smoothies!

One of the great things about smoothies is that you can change them to meet your needs and to create a more balanced meal. There is nothing wrong with making a plain fruit and leafy greens smoothie but if you're looking to get some sustenance and use it as a meal replacement you simply need to add in some fat and protein.

However, fat and protein aren't the only things you can add to your smoothies. If you're feeling adventurous you can elevate your smoothies by adding in different super food and green powders. Even certain spices like cinnamon are great for your health and also enhance the flavor of your smoothies.

Here are some ideas to get you started.

Chia Seeds

This is one of the most well rounded things you can add to your smoothie! How so? Well for starters, there are more omega-3's in a single 1 oz. serving of chia seeds than there are in a serving of salmon. Pretty unbelievable, right? And if that alone isn't enough of an argument, a serving of chia seeds contains a third of the fiber you need for the whole day and 25% of a large portion of your nutrients—including calcium, manganese and phosphorous. Not to mention there are 4.4 g of protein in a serving, making this one addition to your smoothies a complete and satisfying meal.

Hemp Seeds

If there was a single thing I would want to always add into my smoothies, hemp seeds would be it. These wonderful seeds are loaded with nutrients. They are high in protein and also omega 3 fatty acids. The mineral content alone is even on par with some of the greens you put in your smoothies. They even add a nice creamy texture to your smoothie.

Maca

I recommend adding this supplement to your smoothie, only in its gelatinized powder form. The reason for this is because it aids in easier digestion, as the maca powder is slightly heated to prevent the ill effects of consuming it raw. One benefit of Maca powder is that it is very high in minerals that you can't get anywhere else. But the thing that really makes this plant special is its energizing and libido enhancing properties. Just one single serving a day is all you need in your smoothie to see the positive benefits it has to offer.

Green Superfood Powders

If you want to drastically increase the nutritional value of your daily smoothie, then these powders are a must. Especially if you aren't adding many greens to your smoothie to begin with. There are many different types of superfood plants like spirulina, chlorella and many different types of green vegetables. By adding the recommended serving of one of these powders to your smoothie is an easy way to get much needed dose of nutrients into your diet without having to eat as many vegetables.

Coconut Oil

This is one of my favourite supplements and I use it not just in my smoothies but even for cooking and baking. Not to mention it has great moisturizing properties so it is my daily skin moisturizer as well. Coconut oil also provides antibacterial and antimicrobial properties and is a wonderful addition to your smoothie if you want clean burning energy that keeps you going strong for hours. The reason for this is because the medium-chain triglycerides also aid in weight loss since they give you increased energy and more of a daily calorie burn.

These are just the five main supplements that I recommend and use on a regular basis. You have many other options, including, but not limited to: goji powder, acai powder, camu camu, cacao, flax seeds, etc. But don't forget that the most important part of a smoothie will always be the fresh fruits and vegetables!

Chapter 6: Words of Wisdom

Drinking smoothies is by far one of the best thing you can do for your health as far as I am concerned. However, like most good things, it is surprisingly easy to abuse. Smoothies are often tasty yes, but in a bid to make them that much tastier, we toss in things that in the long run, make it harder to keep the weight off. A few lifestyle adjustments are also necessary. For instance, you could use the herb, tarragon instead of salt because it has a sweet liquorice taste in foods.

Nut Butters

Yeah I know they are tasty and all, but they have a mind-boggling calorie content! If you're like me, peanut, almond and hazelnut butters are those foods that taste so good a little is never enough. Now if that doesn't scare you away from the jar, take a second look at those love handles. I'm not at all saying nut butters are bad, but they should be limited.

I love peanut butter for example, but I try to avoid using too much. Its fat content is entirely omega 6 and unless you're consuming enough omega 3's to balance those fatty acids your health could take a toll for the worse. Stick with tree nuts for a better fatty acid profile and simply more health benefits. But again limit the amount of nuts in general if you're trying to lose weight.

Yogurt

Okay, chill. Not all yogurt attracts a frown when trying to lose weight; I mean some of the recipes in this book could use a little of yogurt. The non-fat, organic Greek yogurt is just what the doctor ordered if you are trying to lose weight. You can use it with your smoothies, but healthy as it is, you don't want to go over the top with it! Just be sure to stay away from 90% of the yogurts out there as most contain a ton of added sugar.

Leaves of nightshade plants

I know I mentioned them before, but they are so dangerous it merits another mention. Three words; avoid, avoid, avoid!

Exercise is king

Smoothies are a blessing in a cup if you're actively working to lose weight. However, while smoothies may be incredibly good for your health and waistline, you'll get even better results when you team your diet up with exercise. The best part about smoothies is that the fruits and veggies used in your smoothies are also major energy boosters. You may begin to find you can workout harder, faster and longer than ever before. This means you'll lose weight and get in shape even faster!

Keep it clean

Hygiene is an important aspect of health. Let's face it, getting sick from preparing your smoothies in a dirty blender will take a toll on your progress and health. No matter what type of smoothie you're preparing, make certain to wash your blender, fruits and vegetables properly! Eating produce not washed properly can cause diarrhea among other more serious issues. Yes, this will make you lose weight but not in a good way. So, just be safe and wash your blender after each use and your produce before blending.

Conclusion

Thank you for taking the time to read this book. You can reach all your weight loss goals by simply learning and applying new healthy lifestyle choices.

If you take the information you've learned in this book and actually put it into practice, you'll succeed in having the body of your dreams. Whether your goal is to lose some inches, become 100 pounds lighter or simply feel younger—you **can** do it!

With the strategies and smoothie recipes you now have, you are definitely on the right path to success.

I wish you all the best and many years of health and happiness.

Remember, never stop striving to become the healthiest and happiest version of yourself. You owe it to yourself to feel happy living in your own skin. Being in a body that you find attractive and that serves you well will bring you so much joy for the rest of your life.

Want more? Be sure to check out my book 'Green Smoothies: 30 Easy and Delicious Green Smoothie Recipes to Boost Your Energy, Lose Weight and Revitalize Your Life.'

Made in the USA
Middletown, DE
30 October 2016